It is Hidaen

Written by Paul Harrison

Collins

Look for it.

The toad is hidden at the bottom.

Can you see it?

The lizard is high up.

Look for it.

This looper moth is on the bark.

Can you see it?

The shark is by the reef.

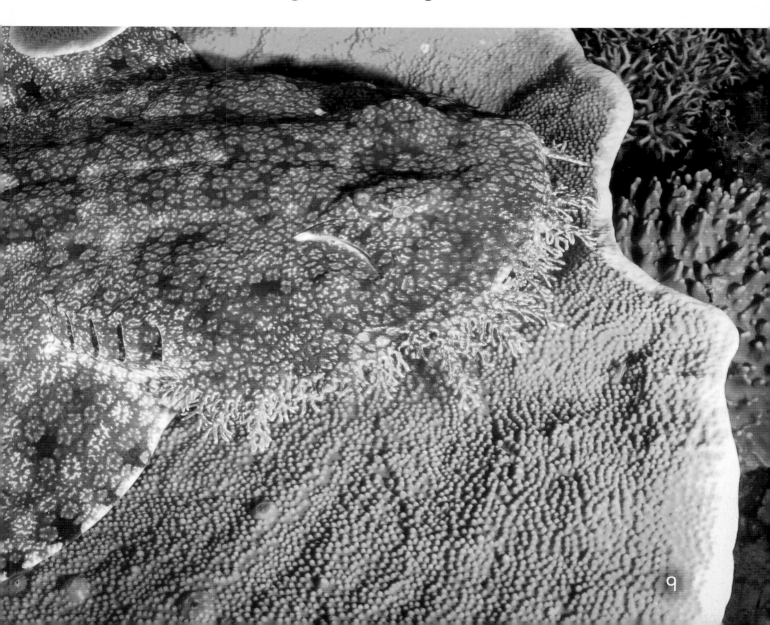

Look for it.

The big cat is hard to see.

Can you see it?

This night owl is hidden.

Did you see?

14

 Review: After reading

Use your assessment from hearing the children read to choose any GPCs, words or tricky words that need additional practice.

Read 1: Decoding
- Practise reading words with long vowel sounds together. Look at the word **toad**. Ask the children to sound talk and blend the letter sounds t/oa/d.
- Do the same with the following words:

  h/igh high   sh/ar/k shark   r/ee/f reef   h/ar/d hard

Read 2: Prosody
- Choose two double page spreads and model reading with expression to the children.
- Ask the children to have a go at reading the same pages with expression.

Read 3: Comprehension
- For every question ask the children how they know the answer. Ask:
  o What sort of place is each animal hiding in? (e.g. *in leaves, up a tree, on the bark of a tree, on the reef, in the long grass, in a tree*)
  o How are the places each animal is hiding different? (e.g. *some are on the ground, others are high up, the reef is underwater*)
  o Which animal did you find the hardest to spot?
  o Why do you think animals try to hide? (e.g. *they are hiding from predators/other animals that might want to eat them or they are hunting for prey/animals to eat*)